THE REIGN: AFRICA

C. NICHOLE

WITH ILLUSTRATIONS BY SAILESH ACHARYA

PAN AFRICAN PUBLISHING HOUSE
DALLAS, TEXAS, UNITED STATES

BOOK DESIGN: C.NICHOLE
ILLUSTRATIONS: SAILESH ACHARYA

PUBLISHED IN THE UNITED STATES BY PAN AFRICAN PUBLISHING
HOUSE.
WWW.PANAFRICANPUBLISHING.COM

PRINTED IN THE UNITED STATES OF AMERICA

ISBN: 9781087917092

AFRICA IN OUR SOUL. WATCH HOW OUR CULTURE GLOWS...

CONTENTS

CONTENTS

LEARN YOUR HISTORY
KNOW YOUR HISTORY
SHARE YOUR HISTORY

PAN AFRICAN
PUBLISHING
HOUSE

INTRODUCTION

The evolution of humans started millions of years ago out of Eastern Africa and down to Southern Africa. All of that happened before people started spreading out all over the world that we know today. Africa is the Motherland of all civilization and forever holds some of the world's richest and most important and sought after resources. Often, we are taught by what we see on television or the internet, not taking the time to learn our own truths and see the beauty from a different perspective, a different outlook. I've had the luxury of meeting some of these tribes firsthand during my many trips to the African continent. I hope that you go into reading this book with fresh eyes and an open mind. I also hope that you want to and will travel to Mama Africa one day. The world is bigger than you think; the world is bigger than you know. Let's learn together...

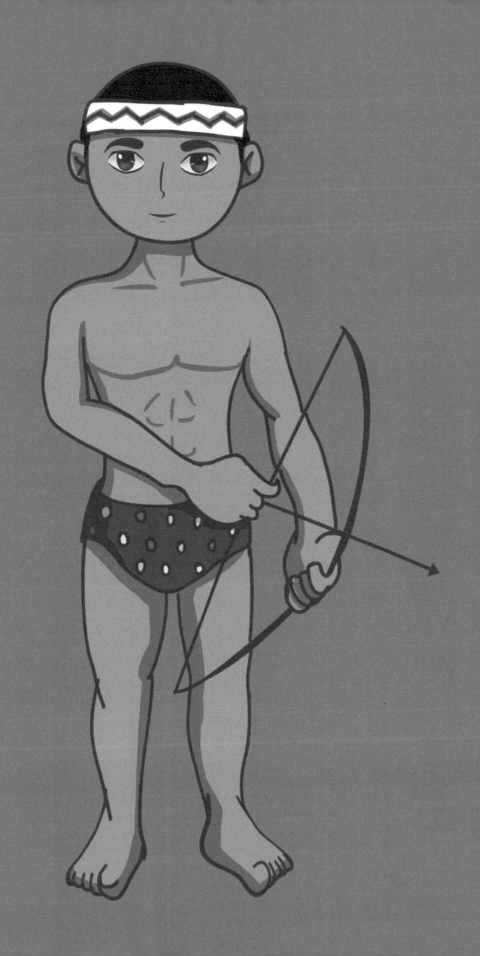

!KUNG

MODERN DAY: ANGOLA, BOTSWANA, NAMIBIA, SOUTH AFRICA
TRADITIONAL LANGUAGE: KX'A LANGUAGES

Many !Kung people are the descendants of those who moved from Eastern Africa into Southern Africa over 150,000 years ago, possibly as early as 260,000 years ago. These hunter-gatherers are one of the oldest cultures on this earth. They live a semi-nomadic lifestyle, moving around seasonally within certain areas, based on what things are available to them, such as water, huntable animals, and edible plants. The !Kung rely heavily on their natural environment.

!Kung men exhibit their strength through hunting animals such as giraffes, wildebeests, antelope, reptiles, gemsbok, and birds. Nothing from the animal goes to waste; blankets are made from their skin, and tools are made from their bones. !Kung women exhibit strength through childbirth. Wanting to be connected with the earth, expecting mothers walk as far as a mile away from their village to deliver their child alone.

Women typically collect water and foods that are high in starch, fruits, berries, and onions. They also usually prepare food and take care of the children. But the !Kung believe in working together equally, so roles are not definite. All jobs are done as needed by whoever can help. Children spend their days playing and having fun. And no matter what age, all !Kung people treat having free-time to relax as a must.

The !Kung take their healing rituals seriously. Having good health is equal to having social harmony, peace, and tranquility. Being a healer is looked at as one of the most important jobs within !Kung culture because healers are greatly relied on to guide everyone psychologically and spiritually through life. The !Kung have been known to say that healing makes their hearts happy, and a happy heart is one that reflects a sense of community.

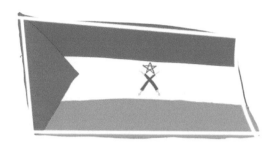

AFAR

MODERN DAY: DJIBOUTI, ERITREA, ETHIOPIA
TRADITIONAL LANGUAGE: AFAR

The Afar live within the Horn of Africa, bordering both the Red Sea and the Gulf of Aden. They also count for over one-third of Djibouti's population. Rulers of the Afar's independent kingdoms are called Sultans. A clan is a group of people who have common ancestors, forming a large extended family. Elders lead an Afar clan, and it consists of two main classes. The Asaimara are the politically dominant class, and the Adoimara are the working class.

Men usually carry a Jile, a curved knife. The Afar men are fearless warriors with extraordinary fighting skills, along with their catalog of tons of battle songs. The Afar don't take to strangers and get hostile towards anyone crossing their territory without permission. If an Afar host offers a guest a drink of milk, and the guest drinks it, a bond is formed. The bond means that the host is now responsible for protecting the guest if trouble appears and avenging the guest's death if they die. On the other hand, the Afar also are big protectors of wildlife. They choose to respect and preserve the environment by trying their best not to harm plants and animals within their territory.

Most coastal Afar are fishermen, while others live a nomadic lifestyle, traveling from place to place to find fresh pasture for their livestock. Pasture is land covered with grass and other low plants that are good for the Afar's camels, goats, sheep, and cattle to eat. Traditionally, the Ethiopian Afar take part in salt trading. Today, the Afar are known to trade butter, animal skins, livestock, and rope for farmers' agricultural goods. Living in areas that contain stone and sand deserts, along with salt lakes and lava streams, don't allow the Afar to grow crops.

It's believed that the Afar get traits such as character and strength from their father, but physical characteristics like height from their mother. The Dayta, or Buttered Curls, is a hairstyle that makes Afar men unique. This look is achieved by slathering butter on a piece of hair and then wrapping that piece of hair around a stick until the curl sets, repeating until all hair is curled. Butter protects the hair from the sun.

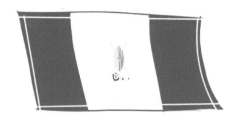

BAGANDA

MODERN DAY: UGANDA
TRADITIONAL LANGUAGE: LUGANDA

The Baganda are the largest Bantu ethnic group native to Buganda, Uganda. The Kingdom of Buganda is the largest of the traditional kingdoms in present-day Uganda. When referring to one person of the Baganda, the term Muganda is used instead. Kato Kintu was the first king of Buganda, reigning in the mid-14th century. Buganda was the largest and most powerful kingdom in the region by the 19th century.

Within the Kingdom of Buganda, clans are significant, and it's a must that everyone belongs to one. Each clan is ruled by a chief, and that chief leads a section of the territory within the kingdom. Clans help the Baganda maintain the tracing of their ancestry. Lineage is passed down through the father. When a Muganda formally introduces themselves, they state their name, the name of their father and paternal grandfather, while also giving a description of their clan's family lineage. It is unacceptable for the Baganda not to know their ancestry and where they fall within it. It is the clan's responsibility to pass on their culture and traditions to the next generations. It is also the responsibility of every Muganda to respect their culture.

The Baganda grow an East African Highland banana known as Matooke. It is steamed or boiled and usually served with peanut sauce or meat soups. Insects such as white ants, termites, grasshoppers, etc. are seen as a delicacy. Although eating utensils are available, the Baganda prefers to eat their meals with their hands.

Before woven cloth was introduced, traditional clothing was made from the bark of trees. Barkcloth is made from the inner bark of the Mutuba tree. Once the bark is peeled, it is treated in boiling water, pounded with a mallet, and then stretched and dried.

BALUBA

MODERN DAY: DEMOCRATIC REPUBLIC OF THE CONGO
TRADITIONAL LANGUAGE: CILUBÀ, TSHILUBA, KILUBA

The Baluba's society and culture dates back to the 400s. Their well-organized community consisted of woodworkers, potters, crafters, miners, blacksmiths, and other professions. Before the 8th century, the Baluba were already using iron and copper to make objects. Fined crafted utensils and pottery have been found by archaeologists dating back from the 8th and 11th centuries. Villages consisted of homes made of reeds and wattle, living by water supplies such as streams and lakes, allowing them to fish. Dams as tall as 6 to 8 feet high were made by using mud.

Nowadays, the Baluba continue to live close to family, keeping the communal spirit. Agriculture remains important as cassava and corn are widely grown, along with salt-making and raising livestock. Artistry still plays a role as wood carvings and handicrafts are sold at markets.

The religious system of the Baluba includes three categories of spirits. The first are the ancestors that usually come in a relative's dream. The spirits of the ancestors are seen as kind and protective over their living family members. The second is the territorial spirit, whose job is to see that plenty of fish are caught, and plenty of animals are hunted. The third is the Bavidye, which is all the other mighty spirits that can possess humans. Sorcery, which is black magic, is frowned upon and not accepted.

Parents expect to be respected. Children who don't do as such may be struck by illness and misfortune by their spiritual ancestors. People who commit minor crimes are trialed by the family's elders or village judges. The Sacred Chief, along with his counselors, settles the more critical cases. In the past, if the offender was found guilty, a possible punishment included being poisoned by a ritualist.

BASOTHO

MODERN DAY: LESOTHO AND SOUTH AFRICA
TRADITIONAL LANGUAGE: SESOTHO

The Basotho, a Bantu ethnic group, have lived in the Lesotho and South African region since the 5th century. When referring to one person of the Basotho, the term Mosotho is used instead. The Basotho make up 99% of the Lesotho population. With Lesotho's entire borders landlocked by South Africa, it's easy to see why they are also the second largest ethnic group in South Africa. Moshoeshoe I was a local chief and military leader who became the first King of Lesotho in 1822.

Even though temperatures are pleasant, the mountains of Lesotho sometime get covered in snow. But it's possible to stay warm with a traditional Basotho blanket. The national hat is the Mokorotlo, a straw hat that even appears on the Lesotho flag. Sewing, beadwork, weaving, and pottery making are still popular traditions. Baskets and sleeping mats continue to be woven by hand from grass. Praise poems and folktales are a tradition that the Basotho hold to heart. Praise poems recount heroic real-life adventures of ancestors or political leaders. Folktales are also adventure stories, but they can be realistic and magical.

Cattle and growing grains such as sorghum used to be an important part of the economy. Now maize (corn), which can be eaten in the form of a thick paste, and bread are the primary foods. Chicken, beef, and lamb are favorites, while sour milk is often the preferred form of drinking milk.

Children are encouraged to have good manners, be polite, and have a serving heart. Hospitality is expected, no matter how much you have. A Mosotho who doesn't have much has still been known to share their food with visitors. It is assumed that when they visit the visitor, they will be treated the same way.

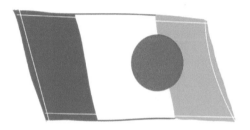

BATWA

MODERN DAY: BURUNDI, DEMOCRATIC REPUBLIC OF THE CONGO, RWANDA, UGANDA, ZAMBIA
TRADITIONAL LANGUAGE: KIGA, KINYARWANDA, KIRUNDI

The Batwa are a Bantu ethnic group native to the African Great Lakes Region that borders Central and Eastern Africa. They are the oldest surviving pygmy people within the region, meaning that they are relatively short, averaging at 5 feet. When referring to one person of the Batwa, the term Mutwa is used.

Being a semi-nomadic hunter is the usual way of life for the Batwa. They think of nature as their mother and father, depending on the rainforest for all of their needs. Instead of gold and diamonds, the Batwa cherish bows and arrows, spears, nets for hunting, and pots for cooking. Providing food to feed their group comes first. The Batwa don't see themselves as poor; therefore, material things like riches don't matter. They consider the rainforest as a paradise. They usually live in a camp from 1 to 5 months, moving after their food supply has run out.

The Batwa considers making pottery to be of cultural significance and an ancestral tradition. It's also a social tradition as digging up the clay and carrying it to their homes allows socializing and bonding time.

Being a community and having respect for one another is what the Batwa live by. They depend on each other, and they share everything. Respect is taught early on to children because anyone within the community is allowed to discipline any child. All women are called Mother because raising every child in the group is seen as a collective effort. The saying that it takes a village to raise a child is a responsibility that the Batwa don't mind having. Children are free to stray into other people's homes whenever and the adults of that home will take care of them as their own. At night, the Batwa like to get around a campfire and tell stories, riddles, and legends.

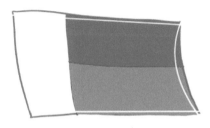

BETSIMISARAKA

MODERN DAY: MADAGASCAR
TRADITIONAL LANGUAGE: MALAGASY

The Betsimisaraka hold rank as the second-largest ethnic group in Madagascar. They are of Bantu African and Asian Austronesian origin. They live among Madagascar's white sandy eastern coastal region, making them excellent sailors, and some were even pirates. Being a fisherman or a whaler is a skill that many pick up, seeing that they have a long history of trading and being upon vessels at sea for long periods. Even in the older days, canoes that could seat 50 or more people weren't out of the ordinary.

Village life revolves around agriculture. Fields are prepared in October by burning off the natural vegetation and planting in the ash-enriched soil. Harvesting takes place in May, with the winter months being from June to September. Rice and vanilla are very popular in the Betsimisaraka economy. Starchy crops such as cassava, sweet potatoes, and taro are grown, along with coffee, sugar cane, beans, peanuts, corn, and different types of greens. Being within a tropical climate region, they get to enjoy the richness of fresh fruit such as bananas, breadfruit, mangoes, oranges, avocados, lychees, and pineapples. Animals play a part too, as the Betsimisaraka catch and sell fish, shrimp, crabs, hedgehogs, wild boars, birds, and insects. Gold and gemstones such as garnet are mined and exported from within the region. Traditional clothing is made from the Raffia palm, which is native to Madagascar. Raffia palm leaves are combed to separate the fibers, then knotted from end to end to form strands that are woven together to create cloth.

Lemurs are held in great esteem as legends are told of these large-eyed and long-tailed primates helping important Betsimisaraka figures in life or death situations. It's believed that the spirits of Betsimisaraka ancestors live inside the bodies of lemurs.

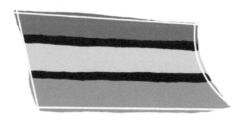

DINKA

MODERN DAY: SOUTH SUDAN
TRADITIONAL LANGUAGE: DINKA

The Dinka, also locally known as the Jieng, are the largest ethnic group in South Sudan, living mostly along the Nile River. Oral traditions state that they have Sudan origins. The Dinka are one of the two tallest people in Africa, with an average height of 6 feet. When young men and women are viewed as old enough to enter into adulthood, their foreheads are marked with a sharp object, creating their cultural scars. The Dinka prefer to experience religion and its power from nature and the world around them, instead of from a thick book.

Cattle are important for meat, milk, eggs, or other products, usually not for profit but for rituals, cultural demonstrations, marriage dowries, bride prices, and many more. A marriage dowry is when the future bride's family gives money, property, or other forms of wealth to the future groom. A bride price is when the future groom's family gives money, property, or other forms of wealth to the future bride. The Dinka grow grain crops such as sorghum and millet for themselves, and sesame, peanuts, and gum-arabic to sell to others.

The Dinka migrate based on the climate. As the rainy season begins around May or June, they move to their permanent settlements that include mud and thatch made houses. The houses are built above the flood level, allowing them to start planting their crops. As the dry season begins around December or January, everyone except the elderly, sick, and new mothers move to their semi-permanent settlements as cattle grazing begins. Dinka women make clay pots and weave sleeping mats and baskets. Dinka men make fishing hooks and spears.

Arguments over which land belongs to who usually don't happen. Dinka land is communally owned, meaning that it is free, and an individual only owns it for as long as they are continually using it. If the land is sold for something such as an ox, understand that the sale is not for the value of the land; it is for the labor that was done to cultivate the land.

DOGON

MODERN DAY: MALI
TRADITIONAL LANGUAGE: DOGON LANGUAGES

The Dogon are known for their impressive mask dances, religious traditions, exquisite wooden sculptures, and architecture.

The highly important Awa society is made up of masked dancers that are responsible for carrying out important rituals. They also are the only people who know the secret language, Sigi So. The Dogon come together so the Sigi can take place. The Sigi is a ritual used to honor and recognize their ancestors. The event starts in the northeastern part of the Dogon territory. Each village takes turns celebrating and hosting luxurious feasts, ceremonies, and festivities. The Sigi is celebrated for about a year before it's the next village's turn, with a new Sigi starting every 60 years. During that time, there will be plenty of new masks carved and dedicated to their ancestors.

The birth of twins is celebrated because it's a reminder of the past when all beings came into the world in twos, symbols of the balance between humans and the divine. For centuries the Dogon have had a system with thousands of signs that include astronomy and calendar measurements, calculation methods, anatomy, and physiological knowledge. They also have had a pharmacopeia, which is a book containing medicines with their effects and directions for their use. Living in harmony is essential to the Dogon and is reflected in many of their rituals. A well-known ritual is when the women praise the men, the men thank the women, the young show gratitude towards the old, and the old recognize the contributions of the young.

Many of the Dogon sculptures are made to be kept private because of the symbolic meaning behind the pieces and the process of which they are made. Only women can make pottery by hand or with the help of a spinning wheel. Only men can make baskets and weave. Only the craft caste can specialize in leather and ironworking. Caste is a hierarchy system that divides society based on hereditary classes, meaning social classes passed down from the parents.

EDO

MODERN DAY: NIGERIA
TRADITIONAL LANGUAGE: EDO

The Edo are descendants of the Kingdom of Benin, not to be confused with the neighboring country of Benin. Formed in the 11th century, the Kingdom of Benin, also known as the Benin Empire, was one of the oldest developed kingdoms in Western Africa. They were praised for their art of brass and ivory, and their sophisticated political organization. Even in the 15th century, when a guest entered the capital of Benin City, they would see a huge palace with many different parts that included courtyards, halls, alters, and passageways that were decorated with brass, ivory, and wooden sculptures. It's never been hard to recognize the Edo people, as they have one of the most elaborate traditional clothing out of all of Africa. Beads, bangles, anklets, body marks, and Raffia work are only scratching the surface of their eye-catching attire.

Forty percent of the Edo State is forest reserves. However, it still leaves enough land for agriculture, which keeps the economy going. Cassava, yams, taro, plantains, okra, beans, rice, pepper, and gourds (pumpkin, squash, cucumber, etc.) are popular crops. The African Oil Palm tree and the Kola tree are essential as well. Oil palm can be found in soap, make-up, ice cream, bread, etc. The Kola tree, which is native to Western Africa, bear kola nuts that contain caffeine and are used to flavor beverages. When it comes to meats that are eaten, goat, sheep, dog, cattle, and chicken are preferred.

In the Kingdom of Benin, the king owned all the land. He could take away land rights if someone committed a crime against the government or betrayed the country. The king appointed all the chiefs. Organized into three main orders, they were the seven Uzama (high ranking chiefs), the palace chiefs, and the town chiefs. Wealth was gained by the king through a monopoly, meaning he held all control over pepper, ivory, and other exports. He also controlled markets and trade routes, opening and closing them as he saw fit. Today, the king's powers have eased as he helps to grant building sites in Benin City and oversees the use of land and resources by foreigners in the Edo state.

EWE

MODERN DAY: BENIN, GHANA, TOGO
TRADITIONAL LANGUAGE: EWE

It's believed that the Ewe have been living within their region earlier than the 13th century. Most of the Ewe population lives in Ghana. Politically they preferred chiefdoms. A chiefdom is a political organization based on hierarchy within one's bloodline, meaning that senior members of select families are chosen to lead. Known for their strong independence, the Ewe used to be continuously at war with each other. Nowadays, there are chiefs and kings within the different Ewe regions, and unity is valued. Connecting with one another, maintaining a level of community and stability in the village, and continuously building a common culture and language-driven identity across the Ewe people in Ghana, Togo, and Benin take precedence.

Dance and drumming are common throughout the land, tying the Ewe together. It is a must that every member participates, and those who don't are looked at as distancing themselves from the group. It is taken so seriously that if one refuses to join in the festivities, they may not get a proper burial when they die. The Ewe believe that someone is a good drummer because they were given the gift from an ancestor who was also a good drummer.

The well-sought after Kente cloth originated from the Ewe. They have a long history of being expert weavers. Kente cloth can be made into any article of clothing, with Ewe chiefs and kings often wrapping themselves in a large fashionable piece.

The Ewe show a lot of respect to elders. They hold so much power that even if a son is married and the head of his household, he is still expected to listen to his father. Land owned by an Ewe family is considered a gift inherited from their ancestors that they are not ever to sell. Folklore, myths, poetry, and songs are plentiful within the Ewe culture and traditions. They are used to teach courage, morals, hard work, life lessons, and wisdom.

FULANI

MODERN DAY: BENIN, BURKINA FASO, CAMEROON, CENTRAL AFRICAN REPUBLIC, CHAD, CÔTE D'IVOIRE, EGYPT, THE GAMBIA, GHANA, GUINEA, GUINEA-BISSAU, LIBERIA, MALI, MAURITANIA, NIGER, NIGERIA, SENEGAL, SIERRA LEONE, SOUTH SUDAN, SUDAN, TOGO
TRADITIONAL LANGUAGE: FULFULDE/PULAAR

The Fulani are also locally known as the Fula or Fulɓe. They are the largest nomadic pastoral ethnic group in the world, traveling from place to place to find fresh pasture for their livestock. They live in Western Africa, spanning across the Sahara desert to Eastern Africa. There are three different settlement patterns of the Fulani. The first is the nomadic pastoralist that moves throughout the year, never staying anywhere for longer than 2 to 4 months. The second is the semi-nomadic, who settles down temporarily during certain times of the year. The third is the settled that has a permanent residence.

Both men and women have tattoos on their faces that were given to them as children. Women use henna for feet, hand, and arm decorations. For young women, indigo inks are also used around the mouth to blacken the gums, the lips, and the area around them. Girls around the age of 2 or 3 years old get their ears pierced, six holes in her right ear, and six in her left.

The Fulani code of behavior is called Pulaaku, and it is passed down from generation to generation. Behaviors that are valued are: patience, self-control, discipline, prudence, modesty, respect for others (including rivals), wisdom, forethought, personal responsibility, hospitality, courage, and hard work.

The Wodaabe is a Fulani tribe that holds a yearly beauty pageant during the Gerewol festival. The men spend hours perfecting their attire and doing their make-up to enhance the features that they believe make a man attractive; white teeth, sharp nose, and a symmetrical face. The goal is for the Wodaabe men to compete by performing the Yaake, a ritual dance. Women judges then select the winner. The winner is chosen by a judge to be her husband. Or the winner has the option of choosing to be the husband of any beautiful woman that he lays his eyes on.

KEMETIAN

MODERN DAY: EGYPT

TRADITIONAL LANGUAGE: ANCIENT EGYPTIAN, CANAANITE, NUBIAN

Kemet, meaning Black Land, can be dated back to 5500 BCE. BCE (before the current era) accounts for all the years before 1 CE (current era), which is today's era. The word Kemet stopped existing when the Greeks colonized the civilization in 332 BCE, naming it Egypt. Colonization is when someone wants someone else's land, so they take it by force without permission, stealing it. Kemetians viewed men and women of all social classes equal under the law. Kemet's law was based on using common sense to decide whether something was right or wrong than only obeying a strict set of rules.

Kemetians have been doing math since at least 3200 BCE, having a completely developed numeral system. Addition, subtraction, multiplication, division, and fractions were a part of everyday life. Calculating the area of rectangles, circles, triangles, and the volumes of boxes, columns, and pyramids were how they planned their construction projects. Basic algebra and geometry were already understood. Pythagoras modeled the Pythagorean Theorem based on Kemetian mathematicians' calculations that they used to improve the stability of the pyramids' walls.

Hieroglyphic writing has been around since at least 3000 BCE. It includes hundreds of symbols representing a word or sound, and the same symbol could have different meanings depending upon the context. Paper was made from the Papyrus plant that grew alongside the Nile river. It helped to have a written language to communicate, especially at the height of Kemet during the New Kingdom in the 1400s BCE. During that time, the civilization included regions of modern-day countries such as Syria, Jordan, Lebanon, Israel, Sudan, and Libya.

Hygiene and appearance were not taken lightly. Kemetians bathed in the Nile River from soaps made of animal fat and chalk and shaved their bodies. Perfumes and lotions kept them smelling good and softened the skin. White linen sheets, made from the fibers of the Flax plant, was the clothing of choice. They also wore jewelry, make-up, and wigs.

MAASAI

MODERN DAY: KENYA AND TANZANIA
TRADITIONAL LANGUAGE: MAA

The Maasai migrated from South Sudan to Kenya in the 15th century. Between the 17th and 18th centuries, they entered into Tanzania. Today, they can be found in the latter two countries within a region known as Maasailand, which has Lake Victoria to the west, and Mount Kilimanjaro to the east.

Herding cattle is a way of life for the Maasai. Herding means bringing individual animals together into a group, maintaining the group, and moving the group from place to place. Cattle are the Maasai's food source; eating their meat, drinking their milk, and sometimes drinking their blood.

The Maasai are warriors at heart with the ability to accurately throw spears 150 feet. The shield and Rungua (wooden throwing club) are also known Maasai Warrior accessories. As a people, the Maasai never thought it was right to have slaves. A slave is a person who is owned by another person, having no freedom, and is forced to obey their owner and work in horrible conditions. The Maasai knew that they wouldn't become slaves and would have their warriors on the front-line to make sure it stayed that way. When people came looking for slaves, they avoided going near Maasai territory.

The initiation into warriorhood, Eunoto, includes singing, dancing, and rituals. During this time, the Adumu, a traditional jumping dance, takes place. The warriors form a circle and take turns jumping. They keep their posture strong and don't allow their heels to touch the ground until their turn is complete. It's not uncommon for a Maasai to jump at least 3 feet up in the air.

Red is the color that the Maasai prefer to wear. They usually have their heads shaven or cut very low. Only warriors are allowed to have long hair, and it's traditionally styled in thinly braided strands. The Maasai pierce and stretch their earlobes, and then add decorated beaded earrings. They all wear beaded and extremely detailed necklaces, with women and girls wearing the bib-like beaded necklaces.

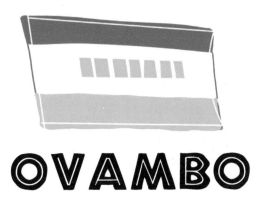

OVAMBO

MODERN DAY: ANGOLA AND NAMIBIA
TRADITIONAL LANGUAGE: OVAMBO

The Ovambo migrated from the Zambia region in the 14th century. During the 17th century, they settled near the Angola-Namibia border, moving further south into Namibia. The Ovambo are a Bantu ethnic group, and also the largest ethnic group in Namibia. In Cunene, Angola (southern Angola), they are known as the Ambo. The areas in northern Namibia and southern Angola where the Ovambo live are sometimes still referred to as Ovamboland.

Herding cattle is the responsibility of the men. Cattle are reputable to have because it shows how wealthy a family is. Kings are known to have the largest herds. The number of cattle other men have varies in size based on their social and economic status. If an Ovambo man doesn't have a herd, it's customary for him to look after another man's herd. Usually, he would take care of a herd that included 40 to 50 cattle, making sure they have good grazing areas during the dry season to get fat quicker. Those men are usually young and not married.

A traditional home has several huts, surrounded by a fence with two gates. Some say it's easy to get lost inside of what seems like a maze. Nevertheless, each hut within the complex has its purpose. For example, one hut is considered the kitchen. Both men and women fish, but it is known for married women to have their own vegetable garden and grain field. Each year, husbands have the duty of clearing the fields for their wives before the planting begins in October or November.

The Ovambo have rituals that have marvelous fire-making ceremonies, throwing herbs in the fire, and breathing in the rising smoke. They also have a rainmaking dance. Traditionally, the king of the tribe was also the head priest. He was responsible for keeping the supernatural spirits company and being the representative of the Ovambo's to the deities. A deity is a supernatural being considered divine or sacred.

TIGRAYAN

MODERN DAY: ERITREA AND ETHIOPIA
TRADITIONAL LANGUAGE: TIGRINYA

The origins of Tigrayans can be traced back to 2000 BCE, with the first mentioning of the ethnic group dated around 525. Aksum was the capital of the Kingdom of Aksum, also known as the Kingdom of Axum or Aksumite Empire, during the kingdom's reign from the 4th century BCE to the 10th century. Aksum is still a part of today's Tigray region that is now known as Region 1 within Ethiopia. Ethiopian tradition states that Tigrayan royalty of the former kingdom can trace their ancestry to King Menelik I. He was the child of Makeda, the Queen of Sheba, and Solomon, the King of Israel.

Handling livestock and agriculture are common jobs for a lot of Tigrayans. Livestock can include sheep, goats, cattle, and even bees. Popular agriculture crops include a native fine-grain about the size of a poppy seed known as teff, and sorghum, wheat, millet, and corn. Typical Tigrayan food contains vegetables and very spicy meat dishes in the form of a thick stew known as Tsebhi. Injera is a large sourdough flatbread made from teff flour. Tsebhi is served on top of an Injera. Tigrayans usually eat food with their right hand, using their fingers as utensils. Since meat and dairy products are not eaten on Wednesdays and Fridays, many vegan meals are available. Family and guests often eat together around a Mesob, a brightly colored handwoven shared food basket.

A Tigrayan house tells a lot about the people living inside of it. A young couple's first house is an average house that they build for themselves, usually a hut with a thatched roof. If the couple lasts, their next house usually is built with bricks, stones, or concrete with a domed roof. Powerful families may later add stone walls around their yard. Guests bring stones with them as gifts of respect to be added to the walls, viewing the walls as a physical representation of the amount of esteem and admiration that the family's friends have for them.

A newborn baby is first recognized as a member of the community during their naming ceremony. These ceremonies take place 40 days after a boy is born and 80 days after a girl is born. If a baby dies before the naming ceremony, no funeral is held for them.

TOUBOU

MODERN DAY: CHAD, LIBYA, NIGER, SUDAN
TRADITIONAL LANGUAGE: TEBU

More than half of the Toubou, or Tubu, population can be found north of the Tibesti Mountains in Chad, with smaller populations in Libya, Niger, and Sudan. Oral tradition says that they originally lived by the Nile River, but left during the 14th century because of a big war. This migration was known as the Kedh Gurrai, meaning the great migration to the south. They are divided into two groups, the Teda and the Dazagra. Toubou means Rock People. They are sometimes called the Black Nomads of the Sahara and are known as the warriors of the desert. The Toubou live in extremely remote areas, meaning very far away from cities. They're so secluded that if a non-Toubou passes through their region, the Toubou will charge them a fee. The religion of the Toubou is Islam, with their leaders being Sultans. But the local herdsmen are the ones who hold the real power.

The Toubou are either herders and nomads or farmers. The nomads herd dromedary camels, donkeys, sheep, goats, and cattle. Livestock is an essential part of trade. Farmers live near oases, where they grow dates, grains, roots, and legumes (lentils, peas, chickpeas, beans, soybeans, peanuts, tamarind, etc.). Salt and natron, which is a salt-like substance, are mined in a few places by the Toubou as well. Those two substances are important because they are used in medicines, soap production, textiles, food preservation, etc.

Not all of the Toubou are nomadic, and some do prefer to settle. Those that settle live in a cylinder or rectangular shaped mud house with a palm-thatched roof. The Toubou society consists of clans, and each clan has individual pastures, oases, and wells. Within the clans, each family has rights to specific land, date palm trees, and wells. Sometimes, a family may even have rights to a part of someone else's harvest from the fields if the water from the family's wells were used to grow the crops.

TUAREG

MODERN DAY: ALGERIA, BURKINA FASO, LIBYA, MALI, NIGER
TRADITIONAL LANGUAGE: TAMACHEQ

The Tuareg are a large Berber ethnic group, known to be descendants of the original Berbers of the Tafilalt region in Morocco, Northern Africa. Their founding queen, Tin Hinan, lived between the 4th and 5th centuries. The Tuareg have been called the Blue People because of their traditional indigo dye colored clothing that stains their skin. Two-thirds of the Tuareg live in Niger. They have been known to be called Mulatthamin or the Veiled Ones. The Tuareg are Muslim, meaning that Islam is their religion.

During the beginning of the 19th century, Tuareg territory was organized into confederations. Each confederation is ruled by a Supreme Chief, a council of elders from each tribe, and clan elders assisting the chief. Every Tuareg clan is made up of tribes, and those tribes are made up of family groups. Throughout history, there have been seven confederations.

The Tuareg are semi-nomadic, known for their tent architecture. These tents have their own styles depending upon the location and tribe. Some tents are covered with animal skin, and some have elaborate mats inside. Traditionally, a tent is put together for the first time during the marriage ceremony and is owned by the wife. For the Tuareg that are settled, their homes are owned by the husband.

A main dish of the Tuareg is Taguella. It is a circle-shaped flatbread made from wheat flour, cooked on a charcoal fire while buried in the hot sand. Once done, the bread is broken into smaller pieces and eaten with melted butter, vegetables, or a meat sauce. About 95% of the Tuareg diet is made up of grains. Dairy such as cheese, milk, and yogurt helps the Tuareg get their protein, as meat is usually eaten on holidays and at ceremonies. Millet porridge and camel's milk with dates are also main dishes. Eghajira is a sweet thick drink that is drunk with a decorative carved wooden ladle and served at festivals. It is made by pounding millet, goat cheese, and dates, mixed with milk and sugar.

WOLOF

MODERN DAY: THE GAMBIA, MAURITANIA, SENEGAL
TRADITIONAL LANGUAGE: WOLOF

The Wolof are the largest ethnic group in Senegal. From 1350 to 1549, the Jolof Empire, also known as the Wolof Empire, was a part of the Senegambia region, consisting of modern-day Senegal and the Gambia. After the Battle of Danki, other states left the empire; from 1549 to 1890, the state of Jolof was known as the Kingdom of Jolof. Culture, caste, and government had been around since the 14th century.

Rites of passage, meaning ceremonies or events marking a critical stage in someone's life, are important to the Wolof. Names are incredibly significant as parents make sure to choose a name for their children carefully. The parents usually pick a name that's a friend or family member who has been influential and has role-model qualities. The naming process can easily take up to a year. It is not uncommon for the Wolof to visit each other whenever they please, even as late as midnight. Spur-of-the-moment visits are not considered impolite or seen as a disturbance. The visitor is encouraged to have tea, share a meal, or spend the night. This Wolof version of hospitality is called Teranga.

At the head of the Wolof caste system was the Paramount Chief, meaning chief of the highest order; then royalty, aristocrats (upper class), warriors, commoners, slaves, and low-status artisans. An artisan is a skilled worker who creates things with their hands. Some professions of the caste system included jewelers, tailors, blacksmiths, musicians, and griots. A griot is a professional storyteller, normally a historian, poet, musician, or entertainer. Most of the Wolof history is known today because of them. Blacksmiths not only made weapons of war, but they also settled local disputes. The Wolof are well-known for their woodcarving, tailoring, and business and trading skills, seeing that they've traded with the Asian Arabs for centuries.

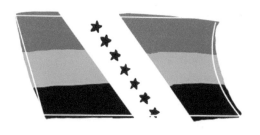

YORUBA

MODERN DAY: BENIN, NIGERIA, TOGO
TRADITIONAL LANGUAGE: YORUBA

The Yoruba originated from The Kingdom of Ife. They eventually started their own empire, the Oyo Empire, from the 7th to the 18th century. The Oyo Empire was very powerful because of its excellent organizational, administrative, and military skills. It was an empire full of wealth and political influence. To this day, the Yoruba are one of Africa's largest ethnic groups.

The Yoruba have always lived in developed cities with large populations. In the earlier times, fortresses with high walls and elaborately carved gates and doors were present. The Yoruba have always been skilled craftsmen, working with leather, textiles, ivory, copper, bronze, brass, ceramics, glass, stone, and carved wood. Yoruba art was also made from the same materials. Their recognized artistic style was very realistic life-sized human sculptures.

The music of the Yoruba people contains a very advanced drumming tradition. The Dùndún is an hourglass-shaped drum with two drumheads connected by leather tension cords. Known as the Talking Drum, the drum can mimic the tone and patterns of human speech's rhythm and sound when played. The pitch of the drum can be changed by the way the drummer squeezes the leather tension cords between their arm and body. Dùndúns are an essential instrument of Yoruba folk music. Caribbean, Afro-Latin, Trinidadian, Capoeira practice music and Afrobeat have all been influenced by the same Yoruba folk music.

Many Yoruba dishes include solid food being cooked by pounding or preparing with hot water, using crops such as yams, cassava, taro, plantains, beans, and corn. Familiar dishes include Moin Moin (bean cake), Iyan (pounded yam), Ewa Aganyin (mashed beans and special sauce), Efo Riro (vegetable soup), Egusi (melon soup), Ila Alasepo (okra soup), etc. The Yoruba diet includes a great deal of Jollof Rice, Fufu, fish, beef, goat, and chicken.

ACKNOWLEDGMENTS

I am always sending so much love to myself! I sat here and did the research, scouted the artist, and wrote the book, so of course, why not? I can't go on without showing my appreciation for the illustrator of the book, Sailesh Acharya. Your work is phenomenal, you understood my vision, and that's all I could have ever wanted. Life is crazy...life is wild! I had people telling me for years that I should write a travel book, and I wasn't feeling it...still not feeling it. But! I saw an opportunity to educate the youth about different ethnic groups. I wouldn't have even thought of that had it not been for my travels. As of 2020, I've been to 93 countries, with 16 of those being on the African continent. Oh, the things my eyes have seen; oh, the experiences that I have had within my 29 rotations around the sun. I just wanted to share a few of those things throughout The Reign series. It wouldn't have been right if I didn't start with Africa. Last, but never least...God. You knew, and you know what was, is, and will be in store for me. I hope, I pray, and I have faith that this book will fall into the hands of children who are the next leaders of tomorrow, who will push the world forward, who will walk in their purpose, and who are culturally aware or will have become as such by the end of reading this book. And if you've read this far, whether you are a child, adolescent, adult or elder, take it as you will, but I want you to remember that it's never too late, nothing's impossible, and you are enough!

ABOUT THE AUTHOR

C.Nichole is a singer, songwriter, television producer, non-profit founder, creative group, and publishing house owner. The Reign: Africa is her first children's book, influenced by the need to have more historical books about African ethnic groups for the youth available, especially for children of African descent. She is also the author of American Presidential Parties: Their Relevance to People of African Descent. C.Nichole is a graduate of the University of Houston, having received a BA in Marketing and Minors in Journalism and European Studies, which included studying abroad in Europe and Africa. She cites herself as being a citizen of the world with 90+ countries under her belt before 30 years of age but makes Dallas, Texas, USA, her home base. She is an advocate for Pan Africanism, uniting all people of African descent, as she is the founder of the non-profit, Pan African Think Tank. You can find out more, donate, and shop apparel at PanAfricanTT.org.

UNTIL NEXT TIME...

CPSIA information can be obtained
at www.ICGtesting.com
Printed in the USA
LVHW072208141120
671375LV00022B/130